ECHOES OF RESILIENCE

TURNING PAIN TO PURPOSE

By Steven Hewitt

Echoes of Resilience
Turning Pain to Purpose

By Steven Hewitt

First published in 2024

ISBN: 978-1-3999-9311-1

Published with the assistance of TAUK Publishing.

To my dad, David Hewitt

Born: 19/11/1948

Passed: 5/6/2022

Your strength, love, and unwavering spirit continue to inspire me every day. This book is a tribute to your incredible journey and the indomitable legacy you left behind. May your story light the path for others as it has for me.

With all my love and gratitude

Contents

Introduction

In *Echoes of Resilience: Turning Pain to Purpose,* read how I navigated the ups and downs of loss and grief after losing my dad. Through heartfelt storytelling and honest reflections, I share how I turned my pain into purpose, finding strength in vulnerability and connection.

This isn't just a story; it's a beacon of hope for anyone facing tough times. With every page, I invite you to witness the power of resilience in action and discover the courage within yourself to overcome life's challenges.

This book isn't about having all the answers; it's about embracing the journey and finding light in the darkest moments. It's a reminder that no matter how tough life gets, there's always a way forward.

Join me on a journey of healing and transformation, and together, let's find our way to a brighter tomorrow.

Steven Hewitt

Why I Wrote This Book?

Echoes of Resilience: Turning Pain into Purpose was written to honour my father's legacy and make a positive impact on people worldwide. Dad's journey with prostate cancer and his unwavering strength and positivity in the face of adversity left a profound effect on me. As I witnessed him navigate his illness with grace and courage, I knew that his legacy deserved to be honoured, and I felt a deep sense of responsibility to share his story with others.

But beyond simply preserving his memory, I wrote this book because I believe in the power of storytelling to inspire and uplift those who are struggling. I wanted to offer a message of hope to anyone who is facing their own battles, whether it's with illness, grief, or any other form of adversity. By sharing my own journey of transforming pain into purpose, I hope to provide practical strategies and insights that could help others find healing and meaning in their own lives.

Moreover, I wrote this book because I believe that we all have the capacity to make a difference in the world, no matter how small or seemingly insignificant our actions may seem. By sharing our stories and supporting one another through life's challenges, we can create a ripple effect of positivity and empowerment that extends far beyond our own lives.

In writing this book, I wanted to contribute to that ripple effect, to add my voice to the chorus of resilience and hope that echoes throughout the world. I wanted to show others that even in the darkest of times, there is always light to be found and that by embracing our resilience and finding purpose in our pain, we can emerge stronger, wiser, and more compassionate than ever before.

The Purpose of This Book

In a world filled with challenges, *Echoes of Resilience: Turning Pain to Purpose* shines as a beacon of hope and inspiration. Through heartfelt storytelling and profound insights, this book takes readers on a transformative journey, exploring the power of resilience and the human spirit.

Written with raw honesty and unwavering courage, the author shares their journey of triumph over adversity. From navigating loss to finding profound purpose, every page brims with wisdom and practical guidance for overcoming life's toughest moments.

But this book is more than just a memoir; it's a roadmap for anyone seeking resilience and renewal. With universal appeal and relatable storytelling, readers from all walks of life will find peace, inspiration, and actionable steps for navigating their own challenges.

At its core, this book is a reminder that within each of us lies the strength to overcome even the greatest obstacles. So, if you're ready to unlock your inner resilience and embark on a journey of self-discovery and empowerment, dive into *Echoes of Resilience: Turning Pain to Purpose* today.

Your path to resilience and purpose awaits.

P.U.R.P.O.S.E.

Passion: Pursue what ignites your passion and brings you joy. Your passion is the fuel that drives you forward, giving you purpose and fulfilment in your endeavours. It's the spark that ignites your creativity and fuels your ambition, propelling you towards your goals with enthusiasm and determination.

Understanding: Seek to understand yourself and your unique talents and strengths. Self-awareness is the key to unlocking your full potential and finding your purpose in life. By understanding your values, interests, and aspirations, you can align your actions with your truest self, leading to greater fulfilment and success.

Resilience: Cultivate resilience to overcome obstacles and setbacks. Life is full of challenges, but resilience allows you to bounce back stronger than ever. It's the ability to adapt to adversity, persevere in the face of difficulty, and emerge from tough times with newfound strength and wisdom.

Persistence: Keep pushing forward, even when the journey gets tough. Persistence is the key to achieving your goals and realising your dreams. It's the determination to keep going, even in the face of obstacles and setbacks. By staying focused and committed to your vision, you can overcome any challenge and achieve success.

Opportunity: Embrace new opportunities for growth and learning. Life is full of them, and each has the potential to lead you closer to your purpose. Welcome new experiences, step out of your comfort zone, and seize the opportunities that come your way. By engaging with change and seeking out new challenges, you can expand your horizons and reach new heights.

Service: Find fulfilment in helping others and making a positive impact. The true purpose is found in service to others. Whether it's through volunteering, mentoring, or simply being there for someone in need. Serving others allows you to make a meaningful difference in the world and leave a lasting legacy of kindness and compassion.

Empowerment: Empower yourself to live authentically and pursue your dreams. Purpose is about living life on your terms, following your heart, and embracing your true potential. Gain personal power to break free from limitations, pursue your passions with confidence, and create a life that aligns with your values and aspirations. By empowering yourself, you can unlock your full potential and live a life of purpose and fulfilment.

This acronym emphasises the components that contribute to an individual's purpose and ability to make an impact in their life. Recognising one's passion, understanding your self-awareness, becoming resilient and persistent in life, seeking opportunities when they present themselves, serving others, and empowering yourself on a deeper level are all key aspects of personal and professional growth.

Chapter 1

What Did I Learn from Dad's Battle with Prostate Cancer?

The sun had just begun its descent on a warm summer evening in September when I received the call that would change my life forever. I remember it with crystal clarity, as if time itself had frozen for that one fateful moment. The voice on the other end was calm but heavy with emotion, and as the words echoed in my ears, my world seemed to crumble—Dad had been diagnosed with prostate cancer.

The diagnosis was like a sudden, violent storm that had appeared out of nowhere, shaking the very foundation of my life. Dad, a symbol of strength and unwavering support, was now facing an adversary he had never prepared for. As his son, I found myself thrown roles I had never anticipated: that of a caregiver, a supporter, and a shoulder to lean on. Little did I know that this journey would teach me lessons that would stay with me forever.

Facing the inevitable

Cancer…

It's a word that strikes fear into the hearts of many, a word that carries with it the weight of uncertainty and dread. In the days following my dad's diagnosis, my family and I were forced to confront the harsh reality of this disease. We found ourselves immersed in a world of medical jargon, treatment options, and the never-ending rollercoaster of emotions that accompanies a cancer diagnosis.

Prostate cancer, the most common cancer among men, had insidiously crept into our lives. It was a silent invader, a thief in the night that threatened the well-being of the man I had always looked up to. Dad, ever the optimist, faced his condition with unwavering resolve. He was determined to fight the disease, to do whatever it took to regain his health. It was in his determination that I first began to see the remarkable strength of what was possible. Dad, who had always been my hero, was now facing his most formidable opponent, and he was doing it with grace, dignity, and an indomitable will.

The shock and emotional turmoil

The days that followed were a whirlwind of emotions. The shock of the diagnosis had left me and my family stunned. We were no longer the invincible unit I had always thought ourselves to be. We were now vulnerable, exposed to a sudden change in my dad's life. Prostate cancer was a formidable opponent, and we were suddenly thrown into a battle we had never signed up for.

I watched as my dad, the man who had always been the embodiment of strength, grappled with his own vulnerability. He was no longer the pillar of invincibility I had looked up to. The emotional turmoil was palpable, but my dad's spirit remained unbroken. He was determined to face the challenge head-on, to do everything in his power to overcome this insidious opponent.

The strength of optimism

As the initial shock began to wear off, I witnessed a transformation in my dad. He had always been an optimist, but his optimism took on a new depth and meaning. He embraced his diagnosis as a challenge, a formidable adversary that he was determined to conquer.

Dad's room at home became a hub of positivity. Visitors, friends, and family were met with a radiant smile despite the pain and discomfort he was experiencing. He joked with the nurses, shared stories of our family adventures, and never let the darkness of cancer cloud his spirit. It was a testament to the incredible power of optimism in the face of adversity.

Lessons in resilience

As the days turned into weeks and the weeks into months, I watched my dad undergo the gruelling treatments that cancer demanded—the pain, the exhaustion, and the uncertainty—constant companions in our lives. But through it all, Dad never lost his sense of humour or his charisma. He showed me that even in the darkest of times, laughter and positivity could be our greatest allies.

It was during this period that I learned the value of resilience. Dad's battle with cancer was a masterclass in tenacity and fortitude. He faced setbacks and complications, but he never wavered in his determination to overcome them. It was a lesson that I would carry with me into the future, a reminder that no matter how daunting the challenges, we have the power to overcome them.

This was the exact reason Dad managed to ring the cancer bell when his PSA level had dropped. His face that day was a picture. It was like he was sticking two fingers up to cancer. It was a very emotional day for the family as our guy had beaten this horrible disease, or so we thought…

The power of love and support

Throughout the course of Dad's treatment, our family rallied around him. We became his unwavering support system, a fortress of love and strength that shielded him from the harshness of the outside world. We celebrated the small victories, the successful treatments, the moments of respite, and the days when the pain was less and we shared the burden of the difficult moments.

Cancer had a way of reminding us of the importance of family and the depth of the bonds that held us together. In the face of a life-threatening illness, the trivial disagreements and misunderstandings that had once seemed significant faded into insignificance. We were a united front, a testament to the power of love and support in the face of adversity.

Throughout this journey, it brought me very close to my auntie, Liz. She had been an incredible support for my dad; whether it involved taking him to hospital to see the consultant, for Dad's ongoing treatments or even a trip down to the pharmacy to pick up the next course of drugs, my auntie was always there. I'll be forever grateful for my auntie's guidance and support through this trauma. She has been not just a rock to my dad but to me too. This made me realise the importance of having quality people around you in your life. We should be making more of a conscious effort in this world to help others.

The gift of time

Amid the chaos and uncertainty, there was a gift that emerged from Dad's battle with cancer, the gift of time. We often take its passage for granted, assuming that there will always be a tomorrow to make amends, express our love, and create cherished memories. But when faced with a life-threatening illness, time takes on a new and precious meaning.

Dad and I spent plenty of quality time together after his diagnosis. We talked about life, our dreams, and the experiences that had shaped us. We reminisced about family vacations, shared stories of our adventures, and laughed about the quirks that made us who we were. In those moments, I realised that time was the most precious gift we could ever receive. It was a stark reminder that life is fleeting, and it's up to us to make the most of every moment.

Back in 2017, Dad surprised me with a holiday to Tenerife. We had the best time together. We would tend to do the normal lad and dad stuff such as afternoon beers as we watched the football, taking part in the activities onsite in the resort and having a laugh with the other guests. With evening meals out and occasionally out on the strip, I think you can paint the picture.

However, this one particular afternoon, we headed out of the resort and about 100 yards away, a shop was renting out mobility scooters. Without hesitation, my dad turned to me and said, "Watch this, Ste,' and approached some guys outside the shop while putting on a limp. After the guys asked for medical records of Dad's injury, which he clearly didn't have, he somehow ended up working his magic, and five minutes later, we were off on a double-seated scooter. It was hilarious, completely spontaneous and as you may know these are how the best stories unfold. We were staying in Costa Adeje at the time, and I took on the driving whilst Dad was topping up his tan on the back seat. We headed to La Caleta for lunch and a bottle of wine before double-backing on ourselves and driving all the way to Las Américas, stopping off at several bars along the way for an ice-cold beer. It was safe to say the ride back was eventful, to say the least.

This was only a drop in the ocean of the memories Dad and I shared, and for that, I feel very lucky to have had such an amazing guy as my dad. He will forever and always be my best mate.

A new perspective on life

Dad's battle with cancer shifted my perspective on life in ways I could never have anticipated. It made me realise the short time of our existence and the importance of living authentically, with purpose and meaning.

The experience of witnessing my dad's journey taught me that life is too short to be spent on trivial pursuits or dwelling on past grievances. It instilled in me a sense of urgency to pursue my dreams, to make the most of my time, and to live a life that aligns with my true passions.

The beauty of everyday moments

As my dad's condition fluctuated, I found myself cherishing the simplest of moments. A shared meal, watching the football, or even a quiet evening at home became precious moments. In the face of a life-threatening illness, the mundane became extra special.

I learned to appreciate the beauty of the every day, the moments that often pass by unnoticed. It was a profound lesson in gratitude, a reminder that life's most precious gifts are often right in front of us, waiting to be acknowledged and embraced.

The journey through my dad's battle with prostate cancer was filled with pain, uncertainty, and heartache. But it was also a journey of profound learning and growth. It taught me about resilience, the value of time, the power of family, and the importance of gratitude. Most importantly, it gave me a new perspective on life and a profound sense of purpose.

This chapter and the lessons it contains have become the foundation upon which I've built the rest of my life. It's a testament to the enduring impact that one person's journey can have on those who love them. In the face of adversity, we discover our true strengths and learn invaluable lessons that stay with us forever. My dad's battle with prostate cancer helped forge my character and set me on a path to honour his memory in the best way I knew how—by embracing life with the same unwavering optimism and resilience that he displayed until his last breath.

Chapter 2

How Did I Cope with the Loss of My Hero?

The passing of my dad on the 5th of June 2022 was a heart-wrenching moment that left an indelible mark on my life. It was as if the sun had been extinguished, plunging my world into darkness. The battle with prostate cancer, which had raged for months, had finally come to an end. It was a sombre ending to a journey that had tested our family's strength and resilience to the fullest.

My hero, my dad, was gone.

The grief that knows no boundaries

The immediate aftermath of Dad's passing was a whirlwind of emotions. Grief, an emotion that has been explored and written about for centuries, is a complex and multifaceted experience. It manifests in ways that are both predictable and unpredictable. In the days and weeks following my dad's death, I found myself engulfed by a tidal wave of sorrow.

Grief doesn't adhere to a schedule or follow a set of rules. It is a deeply personal and often unpredictable journey. Some days, I would wake up with a sense of acceptance and the ability to move forward, while others would be filled with an overwhelming sense of loss. The smallest things would trigger tears, a photograph, a piece of his handwriting, or a certain song on the radio.

The void left behind

The loss of my dad created a void in my life that I could hardly comprehend. He had been more than just a parent; he had been my mentor, my confidant, and my unwavering source of support. His wisdom had guided me through the trials and tribulations of life, and his humour had added lightness to even the longer days. The feeling of emptiness was palpable. The world seemed colder and less welcoming without his presence.

The importance of mourning

In my grief, I began to understand the significance of mourning. Mourning is a process that allows us to express our grief and honour the memory of the one we've lost. It's a deeply personal journey, and there's no right or wrong way to do it.

I found myself seeking solace in simple rituals. I would visit the places where my dad and I had shared so many memories, such as Deepdale, where we used to go and watch Preston North End FC, and the beach on the front at Lytham St Annes, UK, where we used to walk. It was my way of connecting with his memory and reminding myself that he would always be a part of me.

Facing the reality of death

The loss of a loved one brings us face-to-face with the stark reality of mortality. It's a truth that we often prefer to avoid, as it forces us to confront our own limited time we have in this world. The death of my dad was a stark reminder that life is a fragile, fleeting gift and that no one is exempt from its ultimate conclusion.

This realisation was both sobering and motivating. It made me re-evaluate my priorities and question the purpose of my existence. I knew that my dad wouldn't want me to be consumed by grief. Instead, he would want me to embrace life, to pursue my dreams, and to make the most of the time I had left in this world.

The role of support

During this tough period, I leaned heavily on the support of friends and family. Grief can be isolating, but it's essential to remember that we don't have to navigate it alone. The people who care about us can be a tremendous source of comfort and strength.

I was fortunate to have a network of family and friends who were there to lend a sympathetic ear or offer a shoulder to cry on. They provided a safe space for me to express my grief, and their unwavering support helped me cope with the immense loss. This is something I'll be forever grateful for. These guys know who they are, and from me to you, thank you.

The unpredictable nature of grief

Grief is an unpredictable journey, and it doesn't adhere to a linear path. I soon realised that it wasn't something I could simply 'get over'. It was a process that I would have to embrace, allowing it to ebb and flow as it needed to.

One moment, I would feel a sense of acceptance and even gratitude for the time I had with my dad. The next, I would be consumed by a wave of sadness, anger, or regret. The unpredictability of grief was a humbling reminder of the complex emotions that accompany loss.

Honouring Dad's legacy

One of the ways I coped with my dad's passing was by honouring his legacy. I wanted to make sure that the lessons he had imparted and the values he had instilled in me would live on—one of the reasons I'm writing this book. My dad published three books, two based on his business in Quality Management ISO 9001 accreditation and one about his journey with prostate cancer. *The Journey That Changed My Life: From Prostate Cancer Diagnosis to Complementary Therapies and Wellness* by David Hewitt and Michelle Bauduin is available on Amazon.

My dad had always been a supporter of personal growth and education, especially in his professional field, in which he excelled, no question. Dad spent 36 successful years working for BAE Systems, becoming the Quality Director in his time and travelling all over the world. In 2000, he went on to set up his own business, Aragon Consulting Service Ltd, where he went into businesses and helped them become accredited in ISO 9001 or helped them bridge the gap once upgrades were made to the accreditation itself.

He encouraged me to pursue my dreams and never settle for mediocrity. In his memory, I decided to dedicate myself to self-improvement, to keep learning and growing in the ways he had always advocated.

Continuing the conversations

As the grief began to slowly evolve, I realised the importance of continuing the conversations that my dad and I had always enjoyed. The debates about life's purpose, sports discussions, and the sharing of personal stories were an integral part of our relationship.

To keep his memory alive, I began writing notes in my phone, documenting our conversations and the valuable insights he had shared with me. I found comfort in revisiting those conversations and feeling as though he was still a part of my life, offering his guidance and wisdom.

The loss of my dad was a defining moment in my life. It was a journey through the depths of grief, a long journey through the unpredictable waves of sorrow. But it was also a journey of self-discovery, of understanding the preciousness of life and the enduring impact of the people we love.

Coping with the loss of my hero was not an easy process. It was a journey that required patience, self-compassion, and the understanding that grief is a deeply personal experience. It taught me the importance of mourning, the role of support, and the unpredictable nature of grief.

But most importantly, it reinforced the significance of honouring the memory of those we've lost. Dad's legacy continues to guide me, pushing me to pursue my dreams, embrace life, and make a difference in the world, just as he has always encouraged me to do.

The pain of his loss has become a source of strength, a reminder that life is too precious to be wasted and that we must honour the memory of our loved ones by living our lives to the fullest.

Chapter 3

What Were the Last Moments Like?

It was a sombre afternoon when my dad was discharged from Royal Preston Hospital, and the atmosphere in the house was heavy with a mix of anticipation and trepidation. Dad had made a heart-wrenching decision; he wanted to spend his last moments at home, surrounded by his loved ones. It was a choice that came out of a desire for familiarity, comfort, and the embrace of family. Dad's house was in Lytham St Annes, a beautiful part of the UK, which I still visit and take comfort in as we shared memories there.

The homecoming

As I watched the medical team carefully bring Dad into his house, where we had set up his bed and everything he needed downstairs in the front room, I was overcome with a sense of responsibility and a profound desire to make his final days as peaceful and comfortable as possible.

The moment Dad came back home, it was as if a ray of light had pierced through the looming clouds of despair. Dad's house, once a place of laughter and joy, was now transformed into a sanctuary of serenity and love. Friends and family gathered, bringing warmth and support, and we all became an extended network of caregivers, determined to make his last days as meaningful as possible.

My dad was placed in a room that had once been filled with his vibrant energy. It was now a space for quiet reflection, for sharing stories, and for saying the unspeakable goodbyes. The room was filled with candles and photographs of our fondest memories that made life so beautiful.

From the moment my dad arrived home, I knew I wanted to be by his bedside, to hold his hand and offer the comfort of my presence. I could feel the weight of his condition, the fragility of life, and the urgency to make every moment count. I sat on the floor by his side, where I would remain for what felt like an eternity, never once letting go of his hand.

I watched him closely, studying his every breath and movement. His face, once vibrant and full of life, was now marked with the wear and tear of his battle with cancer. This was the hardest thing I've ever gone through in my life, watching the life of your dad, your best friend, slip away. My brain decided to send through all the incredible memories as snapshots we had together as though it was working like one of those old film players. I sensed the inevitable, and I just didn't want to see him go.

The emotional rollercoaster

The days that followed were an emotional rollercoaster. I witnessed the full spectrum of human emotions, the tears that flowed freely, the laughter that was tinged with sadness, and the silences that spoke volumes. It was a time of reflection, of sharing cherished memories, and of expressing our love for a man who had been the cornerstone of our family.

The room became a haven for storytelling, where we recalled the adventures, the mishaps, and the moments that had defined our lives. Dad's battle with cancer had slammed us into a whirlwind of pain, but it had also allowed us to reminisce and express our gratitude for the time we had shared.

The hardest thing I've ever done

As the days turned into nights and back into days, the reality of the situation became increasingly evident. The realisation that I was losing not only my dad but also my best friend was a weight that seemed almost unbearable. As I watched the illness erode his strength and vitality, I couldn't help but feel helpless in the face of his suffering.

One of the most heart-wrenching moments was hearing my dad's laboured breaths. The sound, once so familiar, had become a haunting reminder of the battle he was fighting. It was a symphony of struggle, a stark contrast to the vibrant man I had always known. His strength was fading, and it was a painful experience to witness.

The final moments

In the quiet of the day, as the world around us was busy working, I sat by my dad's side, holding his hand as I had done for days on end. It was a profound and deeply emotional experience, and it brought to the forefront the raw intensity of our connection.

As my dad's breathing grew shallower and more laboured, I knew that we were approaching the inevitable. It was a moment that I had dreaded, and yet it was also a moment that I was determined to face with courage and love.

In those final moments, there was a tangible sense of peace. The room was filled with the love and presence of those who cared for him, and it was as if the universe itself had paused to pay its respects. My dad's struggle was coming to an end, and he was surrounded by the warmth of family and the reassurance of our love.

The hardest goodbye

The moment my dad took his last breath on the 5th of June, 2022, at 15.20, it was a heart-rending experience that words can hardly describe. It was the culmination of a journey that had tested our family's strength and resilience to the fullest. The room was filled with a profound sense of loss, a silence that echoed with the weight of our grief.

I continued to hold his hand, even after his last breath had left his body. It was a gesture of love, of saying a final goodbye to the man who had shaped my life and been my guiding light. The tears flowed freely, as did the memories of our shared moments and the knowledge that I would carry his legacy with me.

The chapter in my life that centred on my dad's battle with prostate cancer, his homecoming, and his passing was a profound and transformative experience. It was a journey that tested the limits of our emotional strength, a testament to the enduring power of love and family.

The experience of holding my dad's hand as he slipped away was a heart-wrenching and deeply emotional ordeal. It was a moment of intense grief and love, a reminder of the fragility of life and the importance of cherishing every precious moment.

My dad's memory continues to guide me, a source of strength and inspiration and a reminder that love transcends the boundaries of life and death.

Chapter 4

What Were the Most Valuable Teachings from Dad?

The passing of my dad left an indelible mark on my life, a void that seemed impossible to fill. As I navigated the emotions of grief and sought to make sense of my loss, I found comfort in the memories of the lessons he had imparted throughout his life. My dad, a man of unwavering principles and boundless wisdom, had left behind a legacy of invaluable teachings that continue to shape my journey.

The power of perseverance

One of the most enduring lessons Dad taught me was the power of perseverance. He was a man who had faced countless challenges and setbacks throughout his life, yet he had never wavered in his determination to overcome them. His battle with prostate cancer was a testament to his unyielding spirit.

I remembered the countless times he had shared stories of his early struggles, as well as the setbacks he had encountered in his career. But through it all, he had never allowed adversity to define him. Instead, he used it as fuel to drive him forward, to become a stronger and more resilient person.

Dad's example served as a constant reminder that life would inevitably present obstacles and hurdles. It was our response to these challenges, our ability to persevere and maintain our determination, which defined our character and ultimately led to success.

The importance of integrity

Integrity was a value that my dad held in the highest regard, and he instilled it in me from an early age. He taught me that one's word was a bond and that honesty and transparency were non-negotiable in all aspects of life. My dad's integrity was a cornerstone of his identity, and it was a quality that earned him the respect and admiration of everyone who knew him.

I recalled the countless times I had witnessed my dad's unwavering commitment to ethical principles, whether in his personal relationships, his business dealings, or his interactions with strangers. He was a man who held himself to the highest moral standards, and he expected the same of those around him.

In a world where integrity could sometimes seem like a rare and undervalued trait, Dad's example served as a constant reminder of the importance of staying true to one's principles and values. His legacy was a testament to the enduring power of integrity, a value that continued to guide my decisions and actions.

The art of empathy

Dad possessed a unique ability to empathise with others, to see the world through their eyes, and to offer genuine support and understanding. It was a quality that had endeared him to everyone he met, and it was a trait that I had always admired and aspired to emulate.

I remembered the countless instances when my dad had extended a helping hand to those in need, whether it was a friend going through a tough time, a stranger experiencing hardship, or a family member facing their own challenges. He had taught me that empathy was a powerful force that could bridge divides, heal wounds, and foster connections.

His legacy inspired me to embrace the art of empathy, to offer kindness and understanding to others, and to seek common ground in a world that sometimes seemed divided.

The value of time and presence

Dad had always emphasised the importance of cherishing time and being fully present in the moment. He often spoke about the need to make the most of every precious moment. It was a lesson that had taken on new meaning in the wake of his passing.

I remembered the countless times he had encouraged me to put away my distractions, to disconnect from the demands of technology, and to truly engage with the people and experiences around me. He taught me that time was a limited resource and that our moments with loved ones were to be treasured above all else.

Dad's journey with cancer highlighted the urgency of this lesson. It had taught me that life was too short to be consumed by trivial matters, that our interactions with others were to be cherished, and that our presence was a gift that we could offer to those we loved.

The resilience of optimism

He possessed an unwavering optimism that had carried him through life's most challenging moments. It was a quality that had become increasingly evident during his battle with prostate cancer. Despite the pain, the uncertainty, and the physical toll of the illness, he had maintained a hopeful and positive outlook.

I remembered the countless times he had shared stories of his optimism in the face of adversity, whether it was a business setback, a personal loss, or a health challenge. He had taught me that optimism was a mindset, a choice we could make even in the darkest of times.

Dad's resilience and optimism had been a source of inspiration, a reminder that our outlook on life could shape our experiences and outcomes. His legacy encouraged me to embrace a positive perspective, to find hope in difficult situations, and to view challenges as opportunities for growth.

The courage to pursue dreams

My dad had always been an advocate of following your dreams, no matter how audacious they might seem. He had encouraged me to pursue my passions and to never settle for mediocrity. It was a lesson that had guided my choices and ambitions.

I remembered the countless conversations we had shared about my aspirations, my career path, and the pursuit of happiness. My dad had been my biggest supporter, pushing me to explore my interests, take calculated risks and embrace change.

His journey had been a testament to the courage required to pursue dreams. Despite the setbacks and obstacles he had faced, he had never abandoned his vision for a better future. His legacy inspired me to remain steadfast in the pursuit of my own goals, to be unafraid of failure, and to persevere with determination and unwavering belief.

The gift of generosity

My dad possessed a generous spirit that extended beyond material wealth. He taught me that true generosity went beyond financial donations; it was a quality of the heart that could manifest in the way we treated others, the kindness we offered, and the compassion we extended.

I remembered the countless acts of generosity my dad had performed, from offering a helping hand to a neighbour in need to lending a sympathetic ear to a friend who faced a challenge. He taught me that generosity was a gift we could share with the world and that it had the power to create a ripple effect of goodwill.

In a society often driven by self-interest, Dad's legacy was a reminder of the value of giving to others. It inspired me to practise kindness, to be compassionate, and to find opportunities to make a positive difference in the lives of those around me.

The impact of family and relationships

My dad always placed a profound emphasis on the importance of family and relationships. He taught me that our connections with loved ones were among life's greatest treasures and that they were to be nurtured and cherished.

I remember the countless family gatherings, celebrations, and shared moments that had filled our lives. My dad had been the heart of our family, the one who had brought us together and fostered a sense of unity and belonging. He used to 'own' Boxing Day. The family would end up at my dad's, and he designed a board emulating the famous game by Bruce Forsyth's *Play Your Cards*

Right. My parents were actually on the real show. Despite answering all the questions correctly, they lost on the board! There was another game my dad designed for Boxing Day, which included fifty-two £1 gifts from Poundland (where nothing is actually £1). These were wrapped and placed in the middle of a table. Everyone was dealt roughly three or four cards each. If my dad turned over your card using a separate deck of playing cards, you would get the chance to pick a gift from the table or steal an opened present from a family member. I remember one year we were all fighting over just one specific present, which was a USB light you could plug into your laptop. It was hilarious!

Dad's journey with cancer deepened my understanding of the significance of family. It showed me that our loved ones are our greatest source of strength and that our bonds with them are to be prioritised above all else. His legacy encouraged me to invest in my relationships, express love and appreciation, and create a supportive and loving network of family and friends.

Dad's teachings provided an abundance of wisdom that will forever guide my path long after his passing. His lessons on perseverance, integrity, empathy, the value of time, the resilience of optimism, the courage to pursue dreams, the gift of generosity, and the impact of family and relationships were invaluable pillars upon which I continue to lead my life.

His legacy remains a source of inspiration, a reminder that his wisdom and values continue to shape my decisions and actions and that his spirit lives on in the lessons he shared.

Chapter 5

What Keeps Me Going After Losing Dad?

A 34-Year-Old's Take

Losing my dad hit hard. No question! It reshaped everything, but I found some anchors that kept me steady. I'm sharing not as an expert but as a friend who's been through it, trying to make sense of life after the storm.

Dad's love: my North Star

His love was a persistent anchor in my life, an unwavering beacon that guided me through the good and bad. He wasn't just a parent; he was a mentor who taught me invaluable lessons about kindness, resilience, and the importance of valuing every person I encountered. Losing him was a profound loss, but it also became a catalyst for reinforcing the lessons he instilled in me.

Kindness and resilience were pillars of my dad's teachings. He believed in the power of empathy and compassion, showing me through his actions that a kind word or gesture can make a world of difference. At the same time, he taught me to be resilient in the face of challenges and to persevere when things get tough.

Dad's loss served as a wake-up call to double down on the life lessons he imparted. I realised that embodying kindness, toughness, and a genuine appreciation for others wasn't just a choice; it was a responsibility. It meant living each day with purpose, integrity, and a commitment to making a positive impact in the world.

In navigating life without my dad physically present, I've made it my mission to be the person he would be proud of. This isn't about seeking external validation or impressing others; it's about staying true to the principles and values he drummed into me. It's about embodying integrity in every decision and action, knowing that his legacy lives on through the way I conduct myself.

If you're reading this and grappling with the loss of a loved one, particularly a parent, I offer this insight: cherish the lessons they taught you. Whether it's kindness, resilience, humility, or any other virtue, these lessons serve as a roadmap for navigating life's challenges and joys. Honour their legacy by embodying those values in your daily interactions and decisions.

In times of hardship or uncertainty, reflect on the principles your loved one instilled in you. Let their love and teachings serve as your 'North Star', guiding you towards integrity, compassion, and purpose. Remember, it's not about perfection but about progress, striving each day to live in alignment with the values that define you.

Moreover, don't be afraid to seek support and guidance from others who share your journey. Surround yourself with a community of understanding and empathy where you can freely express your thoughts and emotions. Together, we can find comfort in honouring the legacies of those we've lost and carrying forward their wisdom and love into the future.

Memories are gold

Memories are not just snapshots frozen in time; they are living threads that weave the fabric of our lives, connecting us to cherished moments, loved ones, and the essence of who we are. As I reflect on the profound impact of memories in my life, particularly those intertwined with my dad, I realise their fundamental value both internally and emotionally.

Memories run deep, reaching into the core of our being and stirring emotions. They are not bound by physical presence but resonate within us, shaping our perspectives, values, and sense of identity. My memories with Dad are a reservoir of laughter, lessons, and love, something I will always hold forever dear to me.

Memories serve as a lifeline that connects me to my dad, even in his physical absence. They allow me to revisit shared experiences, conversations, and moments of bonding, keeping his spirit alive in my heart. Each memory is a benchmark of our relationship, offering comfort, inspiration, and a sense of continuity.

When I share these stories with others, it's not just about reminiscing; it's about spreading joy, wisdom, and connection. Memories have a ripple effect, touching the lives of those who hear them and inspiring them to celebrate their own stories. It's a collective celebration of the human experience, acknowledging that we are all custodians of precious memories.

If you find yourself navigating the landscape of memories after loss, I offer this perspective: cherish each memory as a priceless gem in the tapestry of your life. Whether it's a shared joke, a meaningful conversation, or a simple moment of togetherness, these memories are a testament to the depth of love and connection you shared with your loved one.

Find comfort in revisiting these memories, allowing them to evoke emotions, laughter, and even tears. They are not just reminders of the past; they are companions on your journey of healing and remembrance. Embrace the beauty of memories, knowing that they carry the essence of your loved one's presence within them.

Moreover, don't hesitate to share your stories with others. By sharing, you not only honour the memory of your loved one but also inspire others to reflect on their own cherished moments. In a world often consumed by busyness and distractions, sharing stories becomes a way of preserving and valuing the richness of human connection.

As you navigate the journey of grief and remembrance, remember that memories are not burdens to carry but gifts to treasure. They hold the power to bring comfort, laughter, and a sense of continuity through loss. Embrace the currency of memories, as they are absolutely gold, precious, timeless, and infinitely valuable.

I invite you to embrace the joy of reminiscence, celebrate the beauty of shared experiences, and find comfort in the enduring legacy of memories. They are the threads that bind us to our loved ones, bridging the gap between past, present, and future with love, grace, and gratitude.

Mental health is not a buzzword

The aftermath of losing my dad was like riding an emotional rollercoaster without a safety harness. The turbulence of grief was raw, unfiltered, and at times overwhelming. Yet, during the chaos, I made a decision that changed my journey; I decided to get help for my mental health. This chapter is not just about my experience; it's a rallying cry for everyone to recognise that mental health is not a buzzword but a fundamental aspect of our well-being.

Grief is messy. It's not neatly packaged emotions but a whirlwind of conflicting feelings, sadness, anger, guilt, and profound loss. When my dad passed away, I was plunged into a whirlwind of emotions, struggling to stay afloat at times with the grief, and I knew I needed to take action and do something about it.

In the past, mental health was often stigmatised or brushed aside as a 'buzzword'. But through my journey of grief, I came to realise that mental health is not a luxury but a necessity. It's about acknowledging the weight of life's challenges and recognising that it's okay to ask for help. There were moments of vulnerability and hesitation, but I found the courage to take that step. It wasn't a sign of weakness; it was an act of strength and self-awareness.

For anyone who may be reading this and going through their own mental health challenges, you are not alone. It's okay to not be okay, and seeking help is a brave and vital step towards healing. Mental health is not a buzzword; it's a crucial aspect of our overall well-being, deserving of attention, understanding, and support.

Firstly, understand that your emotions are valid. Grief, anxiety, and depression are not signs of weakness but natural responses to life's complexities. Allow yourself to feel without judgment or self-criticism.

Secondly, break free from the stigma surrounding mental health. Open up conversations with trusted friends, family members, or mental health professionals. Sharing your struggles is not a burden but a pathway to healing and resilience.

Thirdly, prioritise self-care. Engage in activities that nurture your mind, body, and soul, whether it's exercise, mindfulness practices, playing your favourite sport or game, or simply taking time for yourself. Self-care is not selfish; it's a crucial investment in your well-being.

Fourthly, educate yourself about mental health. Understanding your emotions, triggers, and coping strategies empowers you to navigate challenges more effectively. Seek reputable resources, attend support groups, or consider therapy as a valuable tool for growth.

Lastly, remember that asking for help is a sign of strength, not weakness. It takes courage to acknowledge when you need support, and reaching out is a proactive step towards positive change. Whether it's therapy, counselling, or simply talking to a trusted confidant, know that there is no shame in seeking assistance.

I will be forever grateful for the impact my coach, Anthony Limon, had on me and continues to do so. I urge you to find yourself somebody you are comfortable with should you feel this could be the path for you. He has helped me navigate through many different aspects of life—both personal and business—and for which I'll be forever grateful. I have included Anthony's details in the back of this book should anybody be interested in connecting with him.

Mental health is a vital component of our overall health and well-being. Embrace your emotions, break the stigma, prioritise self-care, educate yourself, and never hesitate to ask for help. Your mental health matters, and by taking proactive steps, you are investing in a brighter, healthier future.

Helping others through the grief tangle

Grieving is like trying to navigate through a dimly-lit room, uncertain of what obstacles lie ahead. While I don't claim expertise in untangling the complexities of grief, I firmly believe that sharing our stumbling blocks and insights can offer comfort and guidance to others navigating similar paths. This chapter is an invitation to journey together, to be companions in understanding, and to find light in the darkness of grief.

Grief is filled with twists, turns, and unexpected dead ends. Each step feels uncertain, each emotion a tangled web of sorrow and longing. When faced with the loss of my dad, I found myself stumbling through this intricate terrain, constantly searching for a way forward.

Despite not holding all the answers, I choose to share my journey of stumbling and learning. It's a vulnerability born out of empathy, a willingness to extend a helping hand to those grappling with their own grief. In moments of darkness, solidarity and understanding can illuminate the path ahead.

By sharing our stories, struggles, and moments of insight, we create a tapestry of collective wisdom. It's not about having a flawless map but offering glimpses of our journeys as signposts for others. We become guides in each other's grief, lending support, empathy, and the assurance that no one walks alone.

Nobody should feel alone during their journey of grief. While grief may feel isolating and overwhelming, there is strength and comfort in shared experiences and shared wisdom.

Helping others through the grief tangle is an act of compassion and solidarity. By sharing our maps, shortcuts, and stumbling blocks, we create a network of support and understanding that exceeds the isolating nature of grief. Together, we navigate the maze, offering guidance, empathy, and companionship along the way.

As I reflect on my journey after losing Dad, I realise that life is a continuous story, a narrative woven with threads of memories, tears, and unexpected joys. I'm just an ordinary guy navigating this journey day by day, discovering resilience in life's twists and turns. Life after Dad isn't neatly scripted; it's a wild mix of emotions, challenges, and moments of growth.

In sharing my experiences, I hope to offer a glimpse into the universal themes of grief, healing, and resilience. Each of us is writing our own unique story with chapters that unfold in unpredictable ways. Whether our stories align or diverge, there's solidarity in knowing that we're all navigating life's complexities together.

Life after loss isn't about masking the pain or pretending everything is okay. It's about keeping it real, acknowledging the messiness of emotions, and finding strength in vulnerability. It's about being the kind of friend who uplifts others, offering empathy, support, and a listening ear.

If my journey resonates with yours, that's wonderful. If not, that's okay too. We each have our own narrative to live, with plot twists, challenges, and moments of triumph. Let's embrace our stories, find silver linings in the storm, and continue writing our own tale, one that inspires, heals, and connects us.

Chapter 6

Fuelled by Grief: Unleashing Motivation and Determination

Life hit me hard. Losing Dad was a gut-punch, a reality check that rattled the foundations of my world. Yet, in the aftermath of grief, I discovered an unexpected wellspring of motivation and determination. Let's dive into the raw, unfiltered journey of acknowledging the pain, letting grief pour out, and finding a renewed sense of purpose.

Acknowledging the pain: the first step towards healing

The first lesson in navigating the maze of grief is acknowledging the pain. It's tempting to veer into denial, to escape the harsh reality, but as the saying goes, the only way out is through. No shortcuts, no detours. You have to stare the pain in the eye and accept its presence without trying to downplay or explain it away.

Understanding that pain, trauma, and suffering are dimensions beyond our comprehension and it is the healthy first step in the psychological process. It's admitting vulnerability, embracing the rawness of the emotions, and recognising that healing begins with acknowledging the wounds. This isn't about plastering on a smile; it's about standing in the storm and acknowledging the rain.

Letting grief pour out

Like a kettle needs a spout to release steam, we need an outlet for our grief. Enter crying—the release valve for the pain bottled up within. It's not a sign of weakness; it's a necessary part of the healing process. Just as boiling water needs to let off steam, grief needs a way to pour out of us.

Crying isn't about wallowing in sorrow; it's about allowing the emotions to flow. It's the physical manifestation of the internal storm, a cleansing rain for the soul. In a world that often expects us to be stoic, letting grief pour out is an act of resilience and self-compassion.

Moving beyond regret: don't beat yourself up

Regret is a heavy burden, a toxic loop that keeps us tethered to the past. Obsessing over what could have been done differently doesn't foster growth; it only submerges us in the murky waters of loss. Healthy grieving isn't about rewriting history; it's about digging deeper to unearth the seeds of growth. It's acknowledging the pain without drowning in the regrets.

Instead of dwelling on the past, healthy grieving is about exploring how to move forward. The focus shifts from what could have been to what can be. It's a subtle but powerful shift in perspective, one that allows the wounds of the past to become the fertile ground for future growth.

Love that it transcends: recognising that love never dies

In the emotions of grief, there's a whispered truth: love transcends the boundaries of life and death. It's a spiritual connection that outlasts the physical realm. Saying goodbye isn't the end; it's a continuation. It's recognising that the essence of love endures, weaving through the fabric of our existence.

Understanding that love never dies is a profound shift in perspective. It's not about closure; it's about continuity. You're not severing ties; you're acknowledging a lasting bond. This realisation becomes a wellspring of motivation, an affirmation that the love shared is a guiding force, not just a memory.

Honouring love with action: turning grief into purpose

Love—now a delicate force—propels us to honour it with action. What did your relationship with your loved one inspire you to do differently in your future? It's a question that echoes in the chambers of my journey through grief, prompting a commitment to continue the legacy of love.

It's about simple, actionable steps. As you reflect on your loved one, you say, "Whatever it is that you inspired me to do, whatever you stood for, I will continue." It's a pledge to infuse their spirit into your daily life, turning grief into purpose.

In the simplicity of this commitment lies the transformative power of grief. It's not about grand gestures or elaborate memorials; it's about the quiet determination to carry forward the essence of love into your actions, choices, and interactions.

Chapter 7

Lessons from a Corporate World: Soaring High, Nurturing Roots

As I write down these words, I find myself at 36,000 feet in the air, en route to Dubai, a new chapter in my professional journey. It's a journey that bears the imprints of my dad's 36-year-long successful career at BAE Systems. A journey that took him around the world, leaving behind lessons etched in professionalism, organisation, hard work, and a love for diverse cultures.

Roots in professionalism

Dad's career at BAE Systems wasn't just a job; it was a testament to professionalism. He wasn't just an employee; he was a craftsman in his field. As Quality Director, he instilled a culture of precision, accountability, and excellence. The corporate world, to him, was a canvas where professionalism wasn't just a choice but a way of life.

In my own career pursuits, professionalism is vital. It's the commitment to delivering excellence, the diligence to meet deadlines, and the understanding that every task, no matter how small, contributes to the larger picture. The corporate landscape, as I've learned from my dad, is a stage where professionalism isn't just noticed; it's respected.

Organising the masterpiece of work

His ability to organise complex projects, streamline processes, and orchestrate teams toward a unified goal was a masterclass in efficiency. The lesson was clear: organisation isn't just a skill; it's the backbone of success.

As I embark on my own endeavours, I carry the importance of organisation with me. Whether it's managing projects, coordinating teams, or optimising workflows, the organisational melody hums in the background. It's the rhythm that ensures tasks are executed seamlessly, and goals are achieved. My dad had a natural gist when it came to this.

Hard work ethos

Climbing the corporate ladder at BAE Systems wasn't a leisurely stroll for my dad; it was a climb fuelled by hard work, dedication, and a relentless pursuit of excellence. The long hours, the intricate problem-solving, and the commitment to delivering beyond expectations were all threads in the tapestry of his career.

In my own career pursuits, the hard work ethos is a guiding principle. It's the understanding that success isn't handed out; it's earned through dedication and resilience. Hard work, as my dad exemplified, is the currency that buys success in the corporate world.

Wings of travel: nurturing a global perspective

Dad's role as Quality Director at BAE Systems wasn't confined to boardrooms; it was a passport to the world. His job took him across continents, cultivating a deep appreciation for diverse cultures. Romania, a place Dad held close to his heart, left a huge impression on him and a business in Cluj, a large manufacturing outfit that had been one of his clients for many years. I remember when we would video call, telling me he'd taken a team out of thirty people for dinner and the stories they shared over the table. My dad and I loved talking football, and he would often bring me back a football shirt from the country he was in. I'll never forget my Romanian shirt, which I still have today. I can't wait to frame it and hang it up on the wall where it deserves to be.

Now, as I take to the skies to Dubai, the importance of travel as a tool for personal and professional growth isn't lost on me. Exposure to different cultures, markets, and ways of doing business is an invaluable asset. It broadens perspectives, fosters adaptability, and instils a global mindset. These are all essential elements in the dynamic landscape of the corporate world.

Crafting my own aspirations

The corporate lessons from my dad's journey are not just inherited; they are foundations upon which I craft my aspirations. As I venture into new opportunities, the blueprint is a fusion of his wisdom and my ambitions. The dream isn't merely to succeed but to soar high like the airplanes that my dad's career was intricately connected to.

My aspirations echo the drive for excellence, the passion for organisation, the commitment to hard work, and the thirst for global experiences. The goal isn't just a successful career; it's a fulfilling journey that weaves the lessons from the past into the fabric of the future.

This chapter is not just a narrative of my dad's corporate journey; it's a testament to the timeless lessons that continue to shape my own professional career. The corporate world, much like an orchestra, thrives on harmony, precision, and the dedicated efforts of each individual.

As I step into the next chapter, Dubai becomes not just a destination but a canvas for applying the lessons learned from a corporate maestro. The elements of professionalism, organisation, hard work, and a global perspective resonate in the background, guiding the rhythm of progress.

The business world, inspired by my dad's legacy, isn't just about work. It's where hard work and quality come together to make great things happen. As I fly high at 36,000 feet, the corporate world keeps moving forward, blending past experiences, current efforts, and future goals to reach new heights.

Chapter 8

Paying It Forward: A Deeper Dive

My father's support was always there, steady and full of belief in what I could achieve. His legacy is timeless, teaching me to nurture dreams without limits.

Paying it forward is about seeing the hidden potential in everyone around us. It's not just about money or grand gestures; it's creating a space where dreams can grow. This might mean giving advice, sharing what we have, or just being someone's biggest fan. It's knowing that success isn't a limited thing; it's something we can all reach for.

When I think of my dad's support, I remember the times he listened to my ideas, encouraged me to try new things, and stood by me when things got tough. That kind of support isn't just about one moment; it's about being there consistently through ups and downs.

Now, I see paying it forward as my way of honouring my dad's legacy. It's about looking around and recognising the potential in others, just like he saw in me. It's giving back in whatever way we can, knowing that even small acts can make a big difference.

For me, paying it forward means being open to helping others without expecting anything in return. It's about creating a culture of support and encouragement where everyone has the chance to pursue their dreams.

I believe that success isn't a limited resource; it's something we can all achieve if we work together and lift each other up. By paying it forward, we're not just helping others; we're creating a better world for everyone.

A vision for the future: collaborative success and inclusive triumphs

Looking ahead to the future, I envision success as something we achieve together, not just individually. It's important to highlight inclusivity in this vision. Success isn't about one person winning and others losing. It's about all of us thriving and contributing to a diverse tapestry of achievements and, above all, being happy!

When we talk about paying it forward, it means more than just helping others. It's about actively looking for ways to support those whose voices may not always be heard. It's about celebrating diversity and making sure everyone has a chance to succeed. In this vision, success isn't a solitary journey but a collective effort that benefits many.

In our collaborative future, success becomes a platform for lifting others up. When one person succeeds, it opens doors for others to follow. This creates a ripple effect of positive change that spreads far and wide.

Imagine a world where everyone's unique talents and perspectives are valued and encouraged. This is the world we strive for, a place where inclusivity isn't just a 'buzzword' but a fundamental part of how we measure success.

By paying it forward in this way, we're not just making a difference in individual lives; we're shaping a brighter future for generations to come. Together, we can build a world where collaborative success and inclusive triumphs are the norm, not the exception.

The importance of connection: building bridges across differences

In a world marked by divisions, the simple act of talking to our loved ones becomes a revolutionary act of building bridges across differences. It's not just about maintaining relationships within our comfort zones; it's about actively seeking understanding and connection with those whose perspectives may differ from our own.

As we stay connected, we open ourselves up to a wealth of experiences, perspectives, and insights. This expanded connection isn't limited to family or close-knit circles; it extends to the global community. Engaging in conversations with people from different backgrounds, cultures, and ideologies broadens our horizons and fosters a sense of shared humanity.

Breaking the chains of negativity: crafting a resilient mindset

The world may continue to be stained by negativity and anger, but our mindset can be a game-changer. In this extended exploration, let's delve into practical strategies for crafting a resilient mindset that can weather the storms of life.

Mindfulness emerges as a powerful tool. By being present at the moment and cultivating awareness of our thoughts and reactions, we gain the ability to respond thoughtfully rather than react impulsively. Mindfulness is not about erasing negativity; it's about navigating it with a centred and composed perspective.

Additionally, the practice of gratitude becomes a cornerstone of a resilient mindset. Regularly acknowledging and appreciating the positive aspects of life, even in challenging circumstances, creates a mental framework that focuses on abundance rather than scarcity. Gratitude is not a denial of difficulties but a conscious choice to emphasise the blessings amongst the adversities.

Stay connected: the dynamics of meaningful relationships

Let's take a deeper dive into the significance of staying connected and the dynamics of meaningful relationships. It's not just about having a lot of connections but nurturing those connections that truly enhance our lives.

Building and maintaining strong connections requires us to be intentional and actively engaged. It's more than just talking; it's about listening with empathy, communicating openly, and genuinely caring about others' well-being. Meaningful relationships go beyond surface-level interactions; they thrive on authenticity and being vulnerable with one another.

In our busy lives, it's easy to overlook the importance of staying connected with ourselves. Taking moments for self-examination and self-care is crucial within the hustle and bustle. When we prioritise our internal connection, it becomes the solid foundation upon which meaningful external connections can grow and flourish.

Here are the 5 vital skills I believe help enhance meaningful relationships:

1. Empathetic Listening: The Key to Meaningful Connections

One of the essential aspects of meaningful connections is empathetic listening. This means not just hearing what someone is saying but truly understanding and empathising with their thoughts, feelings, and experiences. It's about being present in the moment and showing genuine care and concern for the other person.

2. Open Communication: Fostering Trust and Understanding

Effective communication is another pillar of meaningful relationships. It involves being transparent, expressing thoughts and emotions honestly, and creating a space where both parties feel heard and valued. Open communication fosters trust, builds understanding, and strengthens the bond between individuals.

3. Authenticity and Vulnerability: Building Genuine Connections

Meaningful relationships thrive on authenticity and vulnerability. When we show up as our genuine selves, flaws and all, we invite others to do the same. Being vulnerable means sharing our true thoughts, feelings, and experiences, even when it feels uncomfortable. It's through vulnerability that deep connections are formed.

4. Self-Connection: Nurturing Your Inner Well-Being

Among our external connections, it's crucial not to overlook the importance of self-connection. This involves taking time for self-reflection, practising self-care, and nurturing our inner well-being. When we are connected with ourselves, we bring a sense of wholeness and authenticity to our interactions with others.

5. Finding Balance: Juggling External and Internal Connections

Balancing external connections with internal self-care is key to maintaining meaningful relationships. It's about finding harmony between engaging with others and taking time for personal growth and self-examination. When we strike this balance, we cultivate fulfilling connections that enrich our lives.

In my opinion, meaningful connections are the foundation of a fulfilling life. They require us to be intentional, empathetic, and authentic in our interactions with others. By prioritising both external connections and internal self-connection, we create a harmonious and balanced approach to staying connected and fostering meaningful relationships.

A future shaped by collective upliftment

The vision for the future becomes clearer: a future shaped by collective upliftment, where success is not a private endeavour but a shared triumph. Paying it forward transforms from a concept to a lived reality, where each individual action contributes to the greater good.

In this future, the legacy of support echoes through generations, inclusivity becomes the norm, resilient mindsets prevail, and meaningful connections form the bedrock of a thriving society. It's a future where negativity and anger are met with a mindset shift, and staying connected is not just a choice but a collective responsibility.

As you navigate your unique journey, I invite you to become an active participant in shaping this future. Embrace the ethos of paying it forward in your daily interactions, nurture dreams beyond boundaries, champion inclusivity, cultivate a resilient mindset, and foster meaningful connections. In doing so, you not only contribute to your personal growth but become an integral part of a collective narrative that uplifts and inspires. Together, let's shape a future where success is not just individual but shared and where the echoes of positive actions reverberate far beyond the confines of our immediate experiences.

Chapter 9

Transforming Pain into Purpose: Lessons Learned from My Journey

Losing a loved one or witnessing them battle a serious illness can be one of the most challenging experiences life throws our way. The pain, the grief, the uncertainty, it can feel overwhelming, suffocating, like a heavy weight pressing down on our hearts. But through the darkness, there is also an opportunity for growth, for transformation, for finding purpose in the pain.

In the wake of my dad's passing and his courageous battle with prostate cancer, I found myself grappling with a whirlwind of emotions, grief, anger, and sadness, but also a deep sense of determination to honour his memory and find meaning during the pain. It wasn't easy, and there were days when the weight of it all threatened to drag me under. But through it all, I discovered that even in the darkest of times, there is light to be found, if only we have the courage to look for it.

Turning pain into advocacy

Witnessing my dad's struggle opened my eyes to the harsh realities faced by individuals battling serious illnesses. It ignited a fire within me to help give back. My dad and I also took part in volunteering for the Walnut Group for one of the events they held in Manchester City Centre. Despite going through his battle, my dad would share his journey and the importance of these tests while putting the men at ease. Since the passing of Dad, I've wanted to give back my time to the charity and decided to hold a golf event at my home golf course, Leigh Golf Club in Warrington, in September 2024. We held 100 free PSA tests on the same day, and the money raised was donated to The Walnut Group. By lending my voice to this charity, I hoped to amplify the importance of these tests that we often ignore.

Creating a legacy

My dad was more than just a parent; he was a role model, a mentor, and a shining example of professionalism and integrity. Throughout his successful career in quality management, he approached his work with an unwavering commitment to excellence and a steadfast dedication to his clients. His legacy of professionalism, organisation, and positivity continues to inspire me, shaping the way I navigate both my personal and professional life.

From a young age, I watched my dad excel in his field, effortlessly blending expertise with a genuine passion for his work. He understood the importance of organisation and efficiency, recognising that meticulous attention to detail was often the key to his success. Whether he was managing his workload or liaising with clients, he did so with grace and professionalism, earning the respect and admiration of all who worked alongside him.

But perhaps what I admire most about my dad was his unwavering positivity and his ability to communicate effectively with others. Even in the face of challenges or setbacks, he remained optimistic, approaching each obstacle as an opportunity for growth and learning. His positive attitude was infectious, inspiring those around him to strive for excellence and embrace a can-do mindset.

As I grew older, my dad and I would often discuss his career, sharing insights and lessons learned along the way. I was struck by his commitment to carrying his principles with him in all aspects of life, not just professionally but personally as well. He believed in showing up as the same person in every situation, embodying the values of professionalism, integrity, and positivity in everything he did.

Today, I strive to honour my dad's legacy by embracing those same principles in my own life. Whether I'm tackling a challenging project, nurturing relationships with loved ones, or pursuing my passions outside of work, I strive to approach each endeavour with the same level of professionalism, organisation, and positivity that my dad demonstrated throughout his career.

In doing so, I hope to not only honour my dad's memory but also to leave a lasting legacy of my own, one built on the foundation of his teachings and the values he instilled in me. My dad may no longer be with us, but his spirit lives on in the way I conduct myself each day, and for that, I am eternally grateful.

Finding healing through creativity

In the wake of losing my dad, I found myself grappling with a whirlwind of emotions, grief, sadness, and a profound sense of loss. Amongst the chaos, I decided to take pen to paper and get creative as a means of processing my pain and finding a path forward. It was during this time that the idea of writing a book began to take shape, a book not only to share my journey but also to provide value to others who may be navigating similar challenges.

Through the process of writing, it has provided a way to channel my emotions into something tangible and meaningful. Each word became a stepping stone on the path to healing. As I poured my heart and soul onto the pages, I discovered a newfound sense of purpose. I had a desire to share my story in the hopes of offering comfort, guidance, and hope to others who may be walking a similar path.

But writing a book was just the beginning. I wanted to do more, to give back in a tangible way that would honour my dad's memory and make a positive impact on the lives of others. Inspired by my love of golf and his commitment to helping others, I decided to organise a charity golf event to help raise money for the Walnut Group, which is dedicated to raising awareness for prostate cancer.

As I reflect on the journey that led me here, I am reminded of the transformative power of creativity and compassion. Through writing and talking, I found healing. Through giving back, I found purpose. Through it all, I discovered that even in our darkest moments, there is light to be found, hope to be shared, and healing to be embraced.

Moving forward, I am committed to continuing this journey of healing and giving back, knowing that in doing so, I am not only honouring my dad's memory but also making a meaningful difference in the lives of others. For me, that is the truest form of healing, to turn pain into purpose and loss into legacy.

Supporting others in their journey

Having experienced the profound impact of support and empathy first-hand, I navigated my own path of healing. I felt an urge to pay it forward, to extend the same kindness and support that had been shown to me to others who may be walking a similar road. Drawing from my own experiences, I attempt to offer a glimmer of light to those who find themselves lost in the shadows of grief, reminding them that they are not alone and that there is always hope for brighter days ahead.

Through the simple act of sharing my story and offering words of encouragement, I hope to provide comfort to those who are struggling. I understand all too well the weight of sorrow and the burden of grief, and I want others to know that they do not have to bear it alone.

In reaching out to support others, I find a sense of purpose and fulfilment that transcends my pain and propels me forward on a journey of healing and growth. It is a journey fuelled by empathy and a deep-seated belief in the transformative power of human connection.

As I continue on this path of paying it forward, I am reminded of the words of wisdom that were once extended to me: that in times of darkness, it is the light of compassion that guides us home. And so, I offer my hand to those who may be struggling, my heart to those who may be hurting, and my hope to those who may be searching for a glimmer of light in the darkness.

Embracing life's precious moments

In the depths of grief and loss, it's easy to feel overwhelmed by sadness. Yet, even in the darkest of times, there are moments of beauty and joy waiting to be discovered. I made a conscious effort to seek out these moments, to embrace the simple pleasures that life had to offer.

During a recent trip to Mexico with loved ones, I found myself surrounded by the warmth of the sun, the laughter of family, and the breathtaking beauty of nature. In those moments, I felt a sense of peace wash over me, a reminder that even during hard times, there is still light to be found.

I realised that by cultivating a sense of gratitude and appreciation for the love that surrounded me. Whether it was walking along the beach with my feet in the sea or sharing a meal with family, each moment became a reminder that life, with all its ups and downs, has so much to offer.

Through these simple pleasures, I found moments of healing and peace. I discovered that even during grief, there is still joy to be found and that by embracing life's precious moments, we can find comfort and peace through the storm.

Seeking professional help

For me, the decision to seek professional help was a pivotal moment in my journey of healing. Through a personal development programme I invested in last year, I had the privilege of connecting with a coach whose wisdom and expertise became a huge help to me. Together, we untangled the knots of grief and navigated the rocky terrain of loss with grace and resilience.

In the safety of our sessions, I found the courage to confront my pain, explore the depths of my emotions, and unravel the tangled web of thoughts that weighed heavy on my heart. My coach offered me a listening ear, a compassionate heart, and a roadmap to navigate the complexities of grief with courage and resilience.

Through our work together, I discovered that seeking professional help was not a sign of weakness but rather an act of strength, an acknowledgement of my humanity and a commitment to my healing. With each session, I found myself moving closer to a place of peace and acceptance, embracing the journey of healing with newfound courage and resilience.

Today, I am grateful for the support and guidance of my coach and for the transformative power of professional help in my journey of healing. I encourage anyone struggling to cope with grief or trauma to reach out for help and to lean on the wisdom and expertise of professionals who can offer support, guidance, and hope in those darker times we face. Remember, you are not alone, and there is always help available for those who seek it. I've included Anthony Limon's details in the back of this book.

Honouring your loved one's wishes

Through the fog of grief, it's easy to feel lost, to forget the wishes and dreams of those we've lost. Yet, by cherishing their legacy and carrying forward their values, we can find purpose in knowing that their memory lives on through us.

For me, finding comfort in honouring my dad's legacy became a guiding light in my journey of healing. As I embarked on the journey of writing this book, I took comfort in the knowledge that by sharing his values and aspirations, I was keeping his spirit alive and ensuring that his impact on the world would continue for generations to come.

Each word penned on the pages of this book became a tribute to his memory, a testament to the love, wisdom, and guidance he imparted to me throughout his life. In sharing his story, I found healing, and in honouring his legacy, I found purpose.

Through the ups and downs of grief, I held fast to the belief that by living in alignment with his values, I could keep his spirit alive in my heart and in the world around me. Whether it was through acts of kindness, moments of generosity, or simply striving to be the best version of myself, I knew that I was carrying forward his legacy with every step I took.

In sorrow, I found comfort in knowing that although my dad may no longer be with me in body, his spirit lives on through the love, laughter, and lessons he shared with me. And in honouring his legacy, I found a sense of purpose, a reminder that even in death, love endures, and memories never fade.

Finding meaning in the pain

In the depths of sadness, it's natural to question why we must endure such profound suffering. While the answers may remain elusive, we have the power to find meaning in the pain by using it as fuel for growth, compassion, and positive change.

For me, the journey of finding purpose in the pain began with a simple realisation: that every act of kindness, no matter how small, has the power to make a difference. Whether it's supporting medical research, volunteering in our communities, or simply being there for someone in need, each gesture of compassion has the potential to create positive change in the world.

I made a conscious decision to channel my grief into action, to use my experiences as a catalyst for support. I found purpose in the pain by lending my voice to those who were struggling through similar challenges. As I continue on this journey of healing and growth, I am reminded of the profound truth that while we may never fully understand the reasons behind our suffering, we can choose to find meaning in the pain by using it to create positive change in the world.

Embracing resilience

Resilience isn't about avoiding pain; it's about facing it head-on and finding the courage to keep moving forward, no matter how tough things get. It's about recognising that we all have the power within us to overcome adversity and emerge stronger on the other side.

For me, discovering resilience was a journey of self-discovery, a journey that taught me that resilience is not a trait we're born with but rather a muscle that we must exercise and strengthen over time. It's about learning to lean on the support of others, to draw strength from their love and encouragement, and to keep pushing forward, even when the road ahead seems daunting.

During my darkest moments, the unwavering support of my family and friends carried me through. Their love became my lifeline, giving me the strength and courage to weather even the fiercest moments. Through their encouragement, I discovered that resilience isn't about going it alone; it's about leaning on others when we need help and offering support in return.

As I continue on my journey, I'm reminded that resilience isn't just about bouncing back from setbacks; it's about growing stronger with each challenge we face. It's about finding the silver lining in every cloud and embracing the lessons that come with adversity.

Through practice and perseverance, I've learned to cultivate resilience in my own life, drawing on the love and support of those around me to keep moving forward, even in the face of uncertainty. In doing so, I've discovered a newfound sense of strength and courage, a resilience that empowers me to face whatever challenges may come my way with grace and determination.

Finding hope in the journey

For me, finding hope was a lifeline, a reminder that even in the depths of despair, there is still a flicker of light waiting to be kindled. It was the knowledge that with each step forward, I was moving closer to healing, to growth, to redemption.

I felt that by holding onto hope, I found the strength to keep moving forward, one step at a time. It wasn't always easy, and there were moments when those bad days threatened to consume me. But through it all, I clung to the belief that better days were ahead.

As I journeyed through the storm, I discovered that hope was not just a fleeting emotion; it was a source of courage, resilience, and unwavering faith in the journey ahead. It provided me with a steady hand that lifted me up when I stumbled.

Today, as I look back on my journey, I am reminded of the profound truth that hope is not just a destination; it's a way of life. It's the belief that no matter how difficult the road may be, there is always a reason to keep moving forward, to keep striving for something better.

In the end, perhaps the greatest lesson of all is that even in our darkest moments, there is always hope. By holding onto that hope and allowing it to guide us through the tough times, we can emerge on the other side stronger, wiser, and more compassionate than ever before.

In the face of loss and adversity, it's easy to feel overwhelmed, to succumb to the weight of our grief and despair. But as I've learned through my journey of transforming pain into purpose, there is always hope to be found, even in the darkest of times.

Each of the strategies I've shared: turning pain into purpose, creating a legacy, finding healing through creativity, supporting others, embracing life's moments, seeking professional help, honouring your loved one's wishes, finding meaning, embracing resilience, and finding hope, offers a pathway forward through those tough times life throws at us.

Remember, healing is not a linear process. It's okay to feel lost, to struggle, to stumble along the way. But as long as we keep moving forward, as long as we hold onto hope and keep searching for meaning during our pain, we will eventually find our way through.

So, to anyone who is struggling with loss or facing a difficult journey of their own, I offer these words of encouragement: You are not alone. Your pain is valid, but so, too, is your strength, your resilience, and your capacity for healing and growth.

I wish for you to find comfort in the memories of your loved ones, strength in the support of those around you, and hope in the knowledge that brighter days lie ahead. May you always remember that even in the darkest of times, there is light to be found, if only we have the courage to seek it out.

Together, we can transform our pain into purpose, our grief into gratitude, and our struggles into strength, and in doing so, we can inspire others to do the same, creating a ripple effect of healing and hope that extends far beyond our own lives.

So let us journey forward together, hand in hand, heart in heart, knowing that no matter what lies ahead, we have the power to overcome, to heal, and to thrive. And may the lessons learned from our pain be the fuel that propels us toward a future filled with love, joy, and endless possibilities.

Chapter 10

Where Am I Now?

Growing up, my dad was a pillar of strength. He was the epitome of hard work, dedicating himself wholeheartedly to his family and career. His relentless pursuit of excellence and refusal to succumb to adversity left an indelible mark on me. Little did I know that these lessons would become the guiding principles of my journey through loss and transformation.

In the aftermath of his passing, I found myself at a crossroads, grappling with the weight of grief and the need to find meaning in despair. It was during this period that I made a conscious decision to channel my pain into purpose, to honour Dad's legacy by living a life of intention and impact.

Now, I am embarking on a new chapter in Dubai, a vibrant city that embodies opportunity and growth. Dubai's skyline, a tapestry of modern marvels, reflects a city that has risen from the desert sands to become a global hub of innovation and progress. It is here, among the towering skyscrapers and bustling roads, that I seek to build something meaningful—not just for myself but for a community of individuals who, like me, have faced the loss of a loved one and are searching for a way to transform their grief into strength.

The decision to create a community dedicated to sharing stories of loved ones and supporting each other through tough times is deeply personal. When my dad passed away, I felt a void that seemed impossible to fill. The pain was overwhelming, and I often found myself lost in memories of his unwavering support and the lessons he imparted. It was in these moments of reflection that I realised the power of shared experiences. By connecting with others who have faced similar losses, we can find solace and strength in our collective resilience.

My vision for this community is one of compassion and empowerment. I want it to be a safe space where individuals can share their stories without fear of judgment and where they can find understanding and support from others who have walked a similar path. This journey of healing is not one we have to undertake alone. Together, we can navigate the complex emotions that come with loss and emerge stronger, with a renewed sense of purpose.

Starting this community in Dubai feels like a fitting tribute to my dad. He was always someone who embraced new challenges and sought out opportunities for growth. Dubai, with its dynamic energy and forward-thinking mindset, is the perfect backdrop for this new chapter of my life. Here, I aim to blend the traditional values my dad instilled in me with the modern innovations that the city represents.

As I work to build this community, I am also focused on expanding my digital presence. Through my website, www.stevenhewitt.info, I aim to reach a wider audience and provide resources for those navigating their own journeys of grief and healing. The digital world offers a unique platform to connect with people from all corners of the globe, allowing us to create a network of support that transcends geographical boundaries.

Moreover, I envision a future where this community extends beyond the digital realm. I hope to organise in-person events and gatherings where members can connect face-to-face, share their stories, and build lasting relationships. These events will be an opportunity to foster a sense of belonging and camaraderie, reinforcing the idea that we are not alone in our struggles.

In conclusion, this new chapter in Dubai is more than just a personal journey—it is a mission to create a positive impact in the lives of others. My dad's legacy of hard work, resilience, and compassion continues to guide me, and I am committed to honouring his memory by helping others find strength in their own stories. I invite you to join me on this journey, to share your experiences, and to be a part of a community dedicated to turning pain into purpose. Together, we can build a brighter, more resilient future.

I am excited for the future and the positive impact I hope to make. As I continue to navigate the ever-changing landscape of the digital world, I do so with a renewed sense of purpose and conviction. Every word I write, every course I create, and every life I touch is a step towards fulfilling my destiny and honouring the legacy of the man who taught me the true meaning of resilience—*my dad.*

About the Author

Meet Steven Hewitt, 34. After graduating with a BA (Hons) 2:1 in sports management from Myerscough College, he jumped from Abu Dhabi National Golf Course in 2013 to the renewable energy scene in the UK.

In his late 20s, Steven became a director but faced cashflow troubles, leading to the closure of his company. Learning from this, he dived into Robert Kiyosaki's teachings, understanding the vital role of cash flow in traditional business.

Returning to sales, Steven continued to explore avenues for personal and professional development. With a keen interest in helping others, he ventured into the realm of occupational health, leveraging his experiences to make a positive impact on individuals' lives.

In his latest chapter, Steven has embarked on a bold new journey, relocating to Dubai to seize opportunities in the Middle East. Alongside his ventures in the region, he has now created a new platform on social media, helping individuals around the world overcome adversity.

Driven by a passion for personal growth and a desire to uplift those around him, Steven embodies the spirit of resilience, adaptability, and unwavering determination.

He's also an avid golfer, a Preston North End football fan, and cherishes quality time with family and friends.

Instagram: @stehewitt_

Facebook: @Steven Hewitt

Website: www.stevenhewitt.info

The Walnut Group

http://www.thewalnutgroup.co.uk

Support group based in Preston for men living with prostate cancer. It offers information and emotional and practical support.

Anthony Limon

anthonylcoaching1@gmail.com

impactleadershipcommunity.com

Printed in Great Britain
by Amazon

47021833R00059